Lawrence
Collection
& Slot Machines

LM Lawrence Maxwell Publications

Copyright © 2023 Lawrence Maxwell

All rights reserved.

ISBN: 979-8-3876-5789-4

For the ones who sing in the shower

Table of Contents

Acknowledgements	9
Many Spears	10
Tuesday Morning at the Park	11
The Paperboy	12
Fourteen	13
Read the poem…	15
Spring Poem	16
MacMillan's Clover Farm	17
A Great Summer Tease	18
Immediately Following a Public Restroom Catastrophe	19
Country Apartment	20
Phoenix	21
Dartmouth Hangover	22
Bannockburn Road in Late June	23
We Planted my Grandmother in a Teacup	24
When You're Ready	25
Sixteen	26
Imagine you are underwater	27
Nana	28
The First Honeybee of Spring	29
And Change	30
Please Don't Open Me	31
Second War of the Mind	32
For Mom	33
Poppy's Handshake	34
Unfortunate Magic	35

In Front of the Queen Street Laundromat	36
Taxi Man	37
City Sunrise	38
Collection Plates & Slot Machines	39
Writer's Lament	40
My Winter Mind	41
They Don't See Our Hearts	42
Candle Dream	43
The Loneliest Places	44
Lupin	45
Sitting on a Cold Log as a Chickadee Pecks a Thawing Maple	46
Red-Winged Blackbird	47
Winter Approaching	48
Snow on the Church	49
Boot Camp	50
Island View Diner	51
Via Rail	52
Salt Water Fantasy	53
Oak Island Observations	55
A Pink Sky	56
Memories of Lunenburg	57
Saint John, New Brunswick - July 13th	58
Snow Flowers	59
Puppy Training	60
The Fisherman	61
Captain's Helping	62

Irving Layton's Montreal	63
Sitting at a Picnic Table, Radically Accepting the World	64
Malpeque Bay Before the Wedding	65
Salivating Glance	66
Dead Man's Jury Duty	67
Cleaning Cars	68
Igor the Crow	69
Sea Glass Dogs	70
Beetle on its Back	71
3 AM	72
This Beautiful Life	73
Father's Wisdom	74
Grampy	75
Victoria Park Sonnet	76
When You Became a Tree	77
Postcard House	78
PEI	79
Early May Morning	80
Dandelion	81
Poverty by Choice?	82
Loyalty	83
The Actor	84
For God	85
Twenty Years for Nothing	86
The Farmers	87
Showcase	88
Memories of Wood	89
The Sea Glass Collector	90

The Sound to Soothe the Worried Mind	91
Psilocybin Sonnet	92
Bonshaw Trail	93
The Hunted Crow	94
Beach Bonfire	95
Musical River	96
Milton Acorn's Crows	97
Cry Out for Love	98
Whistling in a Battlefield	99
Admiring You	100
Poetry is	101
An Old Friend	102
Blockage	103
Leaving the Band	104
Evening cigar	105
Island Summer	106
Ego Death	107
The Dunes	108
The Bird	110
Falling Music	111
Winter Closure	112
About The Author	114

4 † $

Acknowledgements

I would like to start by acknowledging the support of the PEI Arts Grants through Innovation PEI that helped to make this book possible.

I would like to thank Brandon Hood and Aidan Searle (hood+searle) for their creative design of this book's cover and layout.

Thank you to Chris Bailey aka "Editor in Chief" for proofreading my manuscript and giving me many great notes, most of which have been implemented.

Special thanks as always to my loved ones for continuing to support my wildest dreams. You know who you are.

"Poppy's Handshake" first appeared in Off-Topic Publishing as the winner of the May 2022 Poetry Prize, with thanks to Marion Lougheed.

"The Sea Glass Collector" and "Falling Music" first appeared in Canadian League of Poets 'Poetry Pause' series – 2022/2023.

"Memories of Wood" first appeared in *Standing Up: An Anthology for Ukraine* (Off-Topic Publishing) - 2023

Many Spears

I want to be alone without feeling alone.
I want to take these nervous phenomena
and balk at their insignificance.
I want to laugh with them and say,
"You're going to need a lot more dirt than that
if you want to bury me."

I am the little boy that never got his paradise.
I am the grown man who has made that peace.
I wish I knew how to cast a healing spell–
I'd let you lick those beaters too.

And don't praise this as excellent–
I'm at the edge of the cliff,
surrounded by many spears.

I am nothing more than everything.
But what good is that right now?

Tuesday Morning at the Park

Inhaling a summer from when I was a boy,
the smell of overhanging leaves
takes me back home.

A man approaches which causes me to jump,
and like the woodpecker, I burrow my body
into a hole where once was a limb.

Who carved this path?
Would I still be here
had they not slaughtered these bodies
for my convenience?

This time, it is a woman wearing sunscreen
who is startled by *me*.
To her, I've kept too still
on a path meant for walking.

The Paperboy

He arose one Saturday morning,
somewhere between
the early days of sore shoulders
and his first sip of beer.

He marveled at how the paper truck
would always have the bundles delivered
before he awoke from childhood dreams,
that were now turning into teenage desire.

He waited until the last minute to get out of bed,
and when it was time, he took his knife out to the driveway,
where he thumbed the dewdrops on the blue garbage bags
and stretched away the plastic to retrieve the bundles
of newspapers held together with white pallet straps.

He packed his bundles like a pro,
bottoms facing upwards and not too full.
His ink-stained hands delivered fresh-pressed news
to every orange juice house on Saturday morning,
where the weekend edition made the burlap sack
heavier than a hockey bag.

After delivering the final paper,
he headed home to pour himself
a bowl of Fruit Loops
and read the comics between bites,
milk dribbling down his chin.

It wasn't long until porch lights from nearby houses turned on
and sleepy arms reached into mailboxes to retrieve
the secrets of the world that he already knew.

Fourteen

I wasn't used to boobs being shown on TV,
or to them being shown at all.
I still had six hundred days before
such flowers were ever offered.

So, I chewed my toast
as pink nipples filled the TV screen,
and two cops raced to capture
the bloodied man who'd abandoned
his truck on the inside of a tree.

My cousin's boyfriend
(who had his drivers license)
said "Let's check it out. You never hear sirens out this way."
And although I'd been enjoying the naked women,
something told me I would find them again.

We piled into the car and raced toward the park
where the flashing red and blue lights
illuminated the Stanhope sky in such a way
I thought possible only in the starless cities
where they filmed *Cops*.

Then we came upon the red pickup truck,
pieces of its windshield embedded in the tree bark.
The sap-covered glass
looked like shattered reflections
of broken leaves.

Police officers searched for the driver
who couldn't have gotten too far.
And we created our own theories
of the man still on the loose,
each more horrifying than the last,
as we drove through the night,
being urged to *move along*.

It was a starlit summer night
in the height of the in-between.
That is, the first time releasing love
and the first time sharing it;
a head-spinning four years
where luck is sparse
and hope is urgent.

Read the poem...

unapologetically;
live in it for a moment,

even after it's over.
Lick your lips

to catch any fallen sugar.
Live with those who you share it with,

here and now,
in the place behind the label

we call the "present moment,"
where even time waits

with an open hand
to receive the bread.

Live with the resuscitated imaginations
of the singers who bring

a teardrop back to life;
their dreams now puppets

with haunted hearts.
You might smile as these words fall,

not because their message is new,
but because even a baby bird

knows what to do
with a worm.

Spring Poem

It's often the moss
that's first to get lost
in the soft intoxication of Spring.
Before the violet crocus
and delinquent flurries
make way for
lavender lilacs
and dandelions.
Where the everlasting crow
and seagulls, white as snow
swallow the sailor's cry.
And what remains
as tides rise
and ships wait
to pass under the bridge?
But a dead leaf
stuck in a spider's web,
rattling against the white birch,
as though a matchbox
stoking the fires of a
child's imagination.

MacMillan's Clover Farm

We were six years old when Frankie's father
gave us five dollars to buy whatever we wanted
from MacMillan's Clover Farm.
Though, it was really to buy himself
twenty minutes alone, as he instructed us
to "read every price tag."

Five dollars opened up aisles of possibilities
as my mother's budget for such things
was only fifty cents on Thursdays.
So, we inspected every orange tag
at MacMillan's Clover Farm,
scoping out the best bargains
which turned out to be bubble gum,
Lime Rickey, and mouse traps.

This was the same place that at the age of three,
my sister snuck in through the front door,
head barely above the counter
where her little hands placed bags of candy
and a VHS tape followed by two words
she heard my parents say to seemingly
never have to pay for anything–
Charge it!

I warned Frankie that such a technique
would not work for us, as my sister
had been *arrested* by my parents.
But our money was accepted
and we hiked through the woods
with our treats, setting mouse traps
and pouring gasoline on the grass,
breathing in the fumes
as we practiced our golf swings.

We were just boys trying to make sense
of what we imagined to be the entire world.
Unsupervised on grey afternoons
in the height of the greatest summer
West Covehead has ever known.

A Great Summer Tease

Unravel your purple satin.
Announce your arrival
with bright orange trumpets.
Emerge beneath dead forest leaves
before the budding green petals
to become sweetened coffee
and early displays of affection.

Sit with every sugared vision,
as acorn caps and mossy banks
entice a roving eye –
I'll liken it to this:

The mainland appears
as a distant blue shadow,
balanced atop glistening stillness.
And swaying dimples spread
like runny porridge
on shoreline rocks.

Oh, my woodland Spring awakening,
I love you sure as birds will sing,
flowers will bloom
and walking dogs will piss.

Immediately Following a Public Restroom Catastrophe

Bulbous willow, witch's wart
Swimming trunks and summer shorts
Little baskets filled with seed
Dogwood branches, roadside weed

Canine tracks on frozen ponds
Wishing wells and magic wands
Move toward a dizzy spell
Summer swelter, hounds of Hell

Distant winds on harbour shores
Dead man's stew, one helping more
Expired love on stone's engraved
Monumental morning shave

Cup of Lady Baker's tea
Deep as each surrounding sea
Forgotten feathers, cherry bud
Colour of the island mud

Bathroom breaks and bookstore walks
Tiny hands on giant clocks
Words that wish to turn back time
Spit out old fermented wine

Second robin, early still
Kick the duck to foot the bill
"What a thrill," I say to you
Let's return in a day or two

and see if anything has changed

Country Apartment

Crickets are louder than sirens
and the valley guides the river toward a listening ear.
Truck drivers have their cigarettes lit
before they leave the parking lot.
And what I thought to be leaves
are forty-odd starlings,
departing the trees like tissue paper
from a child's eager hands.

Phoenix

There's a foulness to shallow falsehoods;
yellow pillow fluff sold as cotton candy,
cigarette smoke disguised as clouds.
On these desolate carnival grounds,
in the deepest puddle, a drowning phoenix
sizzles into wet ash.

Her remains are scattered across city streets
by April winds that save only the big pieces
from cobblestone grout.

The street sweeper gathers what's left
before cleaning the day's milk
from a body they told her
was too powerful to be displayed.

And so, she flaunted every winding curve
through big cities and bad neighbourhoods
in some experimental America,
where forest fires are sold
like the dream we buy
each day when we rise,
and rise
again.

Dartmouth Hangover

Sleeping in the room where the kittens feed
and everyone drinks the sun's yellow tea.
Susceptible to ailments brought in by evening drafts;
kicking them in the guts before they get you.

Dartmouth hangover, less severe than my last,
where the size of my heart was not measured
by the body before me.

It was only in dreams where I faced the storms
that swallowed many good men, that I realized
I too could be okay with drowning.

Bannockburn Road in Late June

The elusive peach lupin
and the roadside mushroom
are making love beside the buttercups,
as an old man looks at me with suspicion
for writing such things.

Down the road, you can smell
the wild roses and clovers
as distant cows moo,
indicating what smells
might lie ahead.

There's a meanness to the dump truck
as it approaches, head on,
passing potato fields
and front yard fountains;
the iron face of a great-grandfather,
who survives to see the child.

All the while, the artists of heaven
paint with dandelions.
Their hard bursts of sunlight folded only
to expose raindrops on their brushes
that wash away the colour of tears.

We Planted my Grandmother in a Teacup

We planted my grandmother in a teacup –
white china with a golden rim.
And we filled it with soil,
leaving enough room for a first sip.

I spoke to her the other day
about doing our part to fatten
the seagulls of Charlottetown
in the late nineties.
I asked if she still holds her breath
when she drives past a Catholic church,
like I would hold mine for the duration
of her cigarette.

I sang to her, and when I did,
I could hear her smile,
as you often can with those
whose laughter is music.

When You're Ready

When you're ready for love,
you'll be intoxicated by raindrops
that fill the wells.
Sparrows will land on your forearm
and you will sing.
Everything will feel right,
even being alone–
you'll be ready for that too.

Sixteen

I visited the park today –
the place we would go
to liberate our brimming adolescence,
opening the door to an
unquenchable thirst, and
learning the true meaning
of the windshield defroster.

The place where you covered me
with a sodden rose
as we rode
into shivering streams
like trail horses eager to swim.

Today I'm sixteen again,
sitting on the cold bleachers,
circling the fields of memories
of tying up the timid purchases
that once held our loving promise.

And I wonder if you've been back since.
And I think of what our eyes might do
if you were to show up here today.

Imagine you are underwater

and the scarcity of breath does not scare you.
And the salt water washes your tired face
as bubbles melt the polished pearls from careful tongues.

Console your eyes and forgive their visions,
for here, the world is not theirs to mend.
Massage your hands and release their bones,
for here, the Earth is not theirs to break.

Surrender to the ocean floor.
Comb the ripples of sand
that exfoliate your hands
and their years of sleep
disguised as dreams.

When you are ready,
ride a bubble through the coral,
never being seen nor touched.
Breach the surface and breathe,
as you bask in the infinite ocean
that now takes your breath away.

Nana

You told me that Milton Acorn once
approached you at a restaurant to say
you had an "interesting face."
And I thought a poet
could have chosen
something more flattering –
though I imagine he was saving his words
for when his heart slowed down
enough for his imagination
to bring you back to life.

But he never knew you
under a sun like this;
you with that glowing summer smile,
pointing to the petunias,
hanging bed sheets on the clothesline,
and handing me a strawberry cake
to share with the men
who never let me win at horseshoes.

He never knew that you walked
between the rows of flowers
as though you were one of them.
Or that any of those men would die happy
knowing that a bowl of your soup
and a cheese biscuit
was his last meal.

The First Honeybee of Spring

Oh, young honeybee,
circling my lemon rosehip tea.
You should be more afraid of me.
But I admire your courage,
blindly following a naive nose for nectar.

You, brash honeybee,
so soon to leave the hive.
Heed my warning,
for though I am a fool,
I am an experienced one!
Twenty-nine winters
I wear under my skin.

Oh, wondrous honeybee,
your hungry thorax pulsates
as you grow timid
of my godly strength
in picking up this mug.

Your greatest martyred attack
is but a minor inconvenience
and a slightly better story to me,
a five-foot six-inch giant.

And Change

In empty valleys
where once lived laughter
and empty pages
that will soon hold scripture,
the imagination runs
like foals in summer pastures.

And lawnmowers
chop the contours
of grassy mounds –
a blade for a blade.

And the word finds me like a lover
who fills the curve in your back
with something exciting and new.

And six yellow mustangs disappear
into dandelion highways
where I imagine
my custom-painted chopper
rides the lightning.

And tourist buses leak money
into rest stop gift shops
before ever seeing the whales.

And teenage hotboxed Hondas
conduct their civic duties
of distraction from
their second-hand predicament.

And such a colour could never be painted,
yet here it is to be enjoyed by all.
The price? Fear.
Exact change only.

Please Don't Open Me

I am the notebook
never meant to be opened,
where you discover more than
sweet bedtime stories
as your eyes betray the pages
never meant to be defended.

I was once a kaleidoscope,
beautiful without meaning.
I was once a refuge for raw meat
before the supermarket displays,
before the bacteria got seared away;
a reminder that every animal eaten
must first be slaughtered.

I was once a soldier;
a brave recruit
before the suit felt
its first drop of blood.
Strong enough to hold my mother
as she cried for a man
I never knew I could be.

But now I'm a collection of careful words,
slumped against broken promises
in abandoned landfills;
a place where flattering gestures
fall into dark holes
and good intentions
are swallowed.

Second War of the Mind

I tickled the pain from last night's pages;
doodles, sketches and one good poem
found in the eye of the storm.
So close to death – words seem
more important than breath.

Milton Acorn once said,
"One man – one war – that's all he's usually good for."
And so, I don the armour from the inaugural battle
where rusted holes let in the cold air,
disguised as bullets.

For Mom

Drifting off with gentle tickles,
and sending me to dream
with your reassuring touch
as if to say,
'I'll be with you all of the way.'
And I've cursed time
for what it's taken from us;
I should thank it more
for what it has given.

I never knew of your suffering
until those same winds called for me.
Then I thought of you
when it reached certain gusts,
and those tears finally came.
I wish they'd have come sooner.
I wish they hadn't come at all.

I see us now, wiping away the soil
as we catch our reflections in passing streams,
admiring the beautiful work of time;
tickled by the Spirit
as we move towards the sun.

Poppy's Handshake

He'd shake your hand as though he were pulling a weed
and when I turned twelve, he taught me how to
see through the soiled promises of earthly negotiations.

His instructions were conveyed in wheelbarrow loads
and his wisdom was a never-ending mist from a bug spray can.
His long grey pants with matching sweatshirt
left only the sight of sun-spotted hands
that gave a fighting chance to many a Spring seed.

Those same hands, he washed with careful intention
as he studied the dirt
that ran down the sides of the white porcelain sink
before trading his sweat for homemade soup
when Nana called us in for lunch.
His silent smile said
such things would always bring joy if you let them.

As I think of him today,
shuffling through the hallways of the nursing home,
my hands are dry with a hundred cuts,
my arms are beds of tiny pink bumps
and my heart carries the blood of the man
whose entire body now waves goodbye.

Unfortunate Magic

In downtown demolition summers,
upper-class parents posture behind their children
like shadows disguised as shields.
Where once stood the run-down old folks' home,
now lives a dusty sky
where pigeons return
to perch on floating particles.

And when I am a shadow, I can see
the others who've been cast into dark corners
while the objects of their desire steal the sunlight.

Imagine those children now in something they've never worn;
the patient garb that waits for their body
to grow into its fabric like a mother's hug,
shielding them from the sun,
and all of its unfortunate magic.

In Front of the Queen Street Laundromat

She had a body that could bear the Earth,
like a turnip on the eve of its harvest.
Her cheeks were ripe tomatoes
and her breasts had been feasted upon
by the mouths of babes and the eyes
of desperate men.

She smelled like a cherry,
plucked from the tree,
and she teased the devil
with tender blue eyes
that held every howling sea.

She walked, wide-eyed, lashes waving t'ward heaven
as though the cement were a cloud of her choosing.
And the sight of her alone
caused a car wreck a day
in front of the Queen Street laundromat.

Taxi Man

His voice appeared well-traveled
Though it was really just worn
Like the tires of his car
Canvasing the same streets for years
Covering great distance
And going nowhere

City Sunrise

Spraying down the entrance
to the laundromat
with a garden hose
as soiled doves smoke cigarettes
through tattooed throats
in daytime alleys.
We all wear the morning
as best we can.

Collection Plates & Slot Machines

I watch as the final three sinners leave the church.
What redeeming words were spoken today?
Perhaps nothing more than a friendly wager
on the number of winter storms
before the chocolate resurrection.

Meanwhile, in a coffee shop basement,
a disheveled old lady
sends the queen on a neon adventure
into the dead sea of chance.

And whose blood will be drunk
at the next communion?
O, father,
lead us well into temptation,
for, spiritual bankruptcy
is the only way to loosen the grip
of the one-armed bandit.

Writer's Lament

Sometimes I wish I had never written a word;
evidence to be examined, and cross examined,
draining the blood from the body of a man
with no choice but to critique his own thorns.
Sucking the joy out with a straw,
rarely moved by art anymore
until something bubbles up, breaks form,
and hardened tears become soft again.
Oh, God, please ignore my empty prayers,
and I'll keep throwing coins into the wishing well.

My Winter Mind

I send my winter mind,
fragile with mirrored ice
into the April thaw.
It's been beaten down
like shifting shale roads
ravaged by wind chill
and many white coins,
each its own denomination.

I send my winter mind,
barely clothed
into a wolf den.
They've had prouder kills
but they circle and sniff
until they realize their intimidation
is wasted on a hopeless gift.

I send my winter mind
through their jaws and throats.
Consumed by fear,
I am a wolf at last.

They Don't See Our Hearts

They don't see our hearts.
To them, we are nothing more
than empty boxes
ready to be crushed
and stacked between dumpsters.

Our disregarded dreams
lie scattered in the sewers of their streets;
those cities from where we've been cast away
for daring to dance during rush hour parades.

Too many eyelids have been closed.
Too many words, erased
by those whose pockets influence
historical amnesia.

They don't see our hearts.
To them, we are nothing more
than waking reminders of their bailed-out failures.
We are the bones that bind their castle walls;
sacrificial self-portraits
haunting the corners of chambers
after evening prayers have washed away
the sins of the day.

We are hungry no more,
as sleep takes us far away
from the people who don't see
our hearts and all of their
beaten treasures.

Candle Dream

I was a quivering candle
that you gently blew to smoke.
You held on to catch the last
of the dripping wax,
not letting one part of me fall.

The Loneliest Places

The glowing blood of orchestras
tingles dark melodies;
a body, decidedly feminine
and a voice that whispers
with the breath of angels.
How can I look away
when her eyes match my own?

The mythology of verse
epitomizes wisdom
through cotton beauty,
resurrected by none,
considered by many
to be worthy of such gifts
that give pleasure
to the loneliest places.

Lupin

To the lone lupin,
bending toward danger
from under the guardrail:
Thank you for the lesson.

Sitting on a Cold Log as a Chickadee Pecks a Thawing Maple

In this stillness,
I will sit with you
to behold
and become
your deepest shadow.

Red-Winged Blackbird

Your chorus plays to fallen willows
as morning sweaters cover
the frozen knots of winter's lashing.

Could it be, that the river runs west
when water longs to be reflected
by twelve o'clock suns
only to be sung
into oceanic slumber
by horizon moons?

Red fields will surely provide this year
if red tape doesn't contaminate
the greatest harvest we've had
since your son was born, Mr. Jewell.

My body aches from reminders
of pretzeled heroics
as a young man with a job.
I was at the whim of someone else's inheritance
and one nail was all it took
to watch the life drain from my foot,
red as the shoulders of the blackbird.

Winter Approaching

The winter and you
approach like
blue hallelujah

Golden band,
frozen in the pond
where hockey sticks
clap for a pass

And goldfish dream
of summer flies
that buzz between
the raindrops.

Snow on the Church

A gentle Spring snow
dissolves the old church,
where pieces of angel pillows
descend and settle upon
sun-worn shingles,
only for the morning
before sinking and thinking
of reincarnation
and ships they've swallowed
and blood they've puddled
and bellies they've nourished
and flowers that have flourished.

My tongue has grown timid
no more do I capture
that childlike wonder.
I watch from my window
the lifetimes of others.
Discover, discover, discover.
Watching this tapestry of tradition
sewn into the hearts of believers.
The gentle Spring snow
sails down my cheek
and dissolves the old church
once more.

Boot Camp

Marching toward the head with Playboys
tucked away in our coveralls,
thinking by now we must be men.
Some walk with deviant confidence
while others shuffle with eyes toward the deck;
everyone reminding themselves how good
life will be on the other side of summer.

It's my seventeenth birthday.
I follow the parade and dodge punches
from repeat offenders,
then eventually give in
to take the licking with a smile,
to show that the Spirit is tougher than
whatever pain guides their knuckles.

Dehydrated cadets narrowly avoid their bayonets
as they pass out on the cement parade square;
the same place where I beat my instructor in a foot race
but lost to a Nigerian girl from our sister platoon.

Today the memory serves me well
as I clean the toilet and whistle
Bohemian Rhapsody.

Island View Diner

These old rocks smell like a young sailor's dream.
The fissures in mountain stone hold the memory
of every thrashing wave that roared long before
John Dunsworth finished his hand-poured amphitheater.

Fried clams waft through the open kitchen window
as rush hour patrons place their order for
rainbow ice cream in waffle cones.

The building is a quasi-lighthouse with a lookout
and no stairs. Two-tone green siding stripped and caked
with second-hand elbow grease.
And a circle window with a frame once thought to be white,
that now wears the years
like a journeyman's hands.

Inside, you'll find your Cindy's and Tammy's
and locals that take advantage of you not knowing
where to place your order.

Via Rail

The guy who assembles airplane parts
got kicked out of the bar last night.
I suppose now might be a good time
to start taking the train.

Salt Water Fantasy

I

I'd like to own a summer home around here,
where women and dogs approach me
and ask what I'm drawing – and I'll tell them
that I outline and shade these very landscapes
with every word I've ever learned.
There's beauty to be built
even if the hammer is your only tool.

I will sit on this bench by the water
where a lonely housewife
on an anchored speedboat
will flash me
while her husband
tends to a broken motor.
I'll send my phone number
via Morse Code, along with an address
to a nearby hotel bar.
And I'll go order a drink
and think about what it would mean
if she were to actually show up.

She can stay beautiful in my mind;
yes, the mind– the safest and most dangerous
place for someone to be,
and maybe tonight, we'd share a fantasy
far away from our commitments to the people
who depend on us to be who we've been.

II

I want to be everything I've ever been, all at once –
the intoxicated dice-roller, born again
for the five minutes that follow love making,
the man running after the horse

that paid the light bill,
and the mime who screams before
the people who paid to see what years
of silence can create.

I'm not noble or wise because
I've never acted out these fantasies;
their presence is evidence enough
of a child's desire to make something
more than the bed.

Oak Island Observations

My chest fills with nothing,
and suddenly there is infinite space
for everything I am.

No more describing the waves,
for they are separate from me,
for they are everything I am.
I am the passing clouds
and the rooted sycamore
sharing a morning in July.

I am the symmetry in the
architecture of beach houses
and the seagull that
sits upon their shingles,
calling to the sailors
who come back home.

I am the man with the
Coors Light backpack,
who later acknowledges
that responding to a "good morning"
wasn't so painful after all.

A Pink Sky

Friday night fishermen
and their high-school sweethearts
are smoking cigarettes on the pier.
They tell me the Prime Minister
was in town today.
But I'm too busy falling in love
with the pink sky.

Open the borders.
Or leave them closed.
Just do something.
Just let everything blur
into the trip
that tickled you most.

Memories of Lunenburg

Eastern Canadian British settlement
with historic houses that sell t-shirts
to retired sailors who've finally arrived
to sail on the Bluenose II.

"For years I've wanted to do it,
and this year my wife surprised
me for my birthday."

I've never felt so close to home
in another village, where the fishermen
are poets and their wives, artists
who paint how they remember the land
before it became a golf course.

Hook-handed pirates wave to me
as Frank Sinatra sings from an SUV
and my foot falls asleep before the chorus.

I sit in the sauna and taste the falling oceans
as they meet my lips.
Parents laugh at their unfunny children
when other adults are present.
And I sit, disgusted and alone,
waiting for my chicken and rice
to arrive, perfectly overcooked.

Saint John, New Brunswick - July 13th

Glenny and I talk about good whiskey
and the Toronto Maple Leafs
as the turkey vultures swarm over the Saint John mountains
waiting for someone else to do their dirty work.

Next, I see the hummingbird, resting for a moment
on the telephone wire as her red-breasted mate
sucks sugar from another feeder.
Their beaks are like wooden stems from flowers
that never spent a moment wishing they could fly.

I have held onto the grouchiness
of the old lady from the pub
for one night too many.

Her: "Pick it up, you're putting us to sleep!"

Me: "Oh, you're sleepy? It must be past your bedtime!"

Her:

*jaw drop
*double middle fingers

In times like these I think of the advice Maharaji gave to his pupil,

"Ram Dass, give up anger."

Snow Flowers

What if in the summer, it snowed flowers?
Purple petals gently fall onto eager tongues,
dissolve into gardens grown within our teeth.
Such a day could halt our destruction
and construction of another needless roundabout,
as taxpayers forget the combination to their own mind.
Forced to watch their demise, they sing,
for a moment, in fields of fallen flowers where even
politicians must throw their heads and hands in the air.

Puppy Training

The girl in the orange sundress
trains her puppy in front
of the government building.

It is a reminder of something
that gets stripped from us
like the phone numbers
dangling from bulletin boards.

That is to say, innocence
can only be taken away.
That is to say, it's hard to sit still
when the whole world excites you.

The Fisherman

The breakwater protects the docks
where drunken men are punched
before falling between the boats.
Chivalry is not dead, though
it is fleeting by the minute.
Even the duck begins to speed
as he departs into the harbour.

One-manned fishing boats
bring in the day's catch
as cigar smoke and diesel fumes
trail behind a yellow beard.
He'll tell you it was not the sun
that brought about his cancer,
though one can never be entirely certain.
But I would never question
a fisherman's logic.

Captain's Helping

What are my words if not flowers in shit?
What good are they if they never bloom?
Love may alter their colours,
liquor may change their shape,
loss may cause them to wilt
and withdrawal may make them tremble
as they regain the rain in their roots,
coming to terms with truth
in the heart punch of some heroic story.

Would you want the Captain's helping if you could choose?
Would you wish for your day with its guaranteed bad news?
Surely a noble war will not go unrewarded.

Irving Layton's Montreal

Imagine Irving Layton sitting here
under a Roman oak tree
with a woman, thirty years his junior.
He writes with a grin only painful to
those who see beyond his academic fortress.
In the same breath, imagine Montreal
might be just the place for you, *bien sur.*
Yes, the sun hits those cobblestone streets
a little harder, like a father who knows his son
will one day be the stronger man.
We all wear our iron chins until time erodes
our metal bones to dust, and we are born again
as glass; beautifully fragile with powers revoked.
In those final days, we will walk, head down
scouring the ground for scraps and paths
that were once maintained by some distant civilization.
In this jungle, there is so much beautiful danger
to which we all must eventually bid farewell.

Sitting at a Picnic Table, Radically Accepting the World

Sunlight makes the sea shimmer
and I shiver.
Light as a raindrop
yet full of the ocean.
Glistening ripples;
quiet fireworks that sparkle
for your birthday.
Distant land faded
into humid diesel air
as trucks idle on the wharf.
Crows and cars
take different roads…

Malpeque Bay Before the Wedding

There are so many beaches where I can go to be alone,
though not completely. The birds still sing from the
yellow houses of dreams. The flies still swarm
the algae-covered rocks as the tide falls back.
The heron still wades in knee-deep water,
stoic as a seasoned fisherman.

The dune trees still whistle, protecting the shores from
underwater screams. The ants still march along
broken slabs of rebar concrete, exploring every
hole on hardened hills. The promise of oysters
still finds the deepest part of my nose.
And not one kilometer down the road,
the bride and groom (to whom I'll sing
for the better part of the evening)
still smile, for they've seen it too.

Salivating Glance

Tie me to the grass and love me.
Or better yet, look at me,
with a salivating glance that holds
every drop of your youth.
Show me how hungry
a body can get.
A true drunk will always take the swig
so long as his eyes are open.

Dead Man's Jury Duty

Tadpoles under the lotus flower;
their little feet emerge
as dragonflies hover in the humid June air.
Dead Man's Pond comes to life
and squirrels become brave.
Leaves, ant-munched, lie hopelessly
beside their rusted brothers
who fell after last summer.

A lone wasp burrows into a toppled birch,
upon which I sit to observe the dog walking his old man.
"Leave it. Leave it. Leave it!" the old man commands.

It's true that, like the dog, I have shat in these woods
while watching Stratford houses become erect
quicker than teenage boys with a Sears catalog.

Cleaning Cars

You never know what you're gonna find
Prescription pills, spare change, or just an old french fry
Dog-hair-covered Timbit from your beach day memory
But I'm tired of living vicariously

Sanity slips between the cracks in the seats
Cracker dust, old receipts, back has aged ten years in three
Dime bags, diaries, devilled-eggs, diapers
Cigarette butts, broken windshield wipers
I could write a whole book on the things that I've found
While cleaning these cars for the people in town

And so, another day passes in this detailer's dream
The grains of sand remind me of time in the clean
And the time in between, deep within a thought
Sometimes that's the best you've got

Igor the Crow

Watching the rain trickle onto roadside lupins,
the crow shakes his feathers from his powerline perch.
With the hunch of his shoulder, he's earned his name.
Perhaps both of us tremble from memories
of Russian vodka, or some other poisonous invasion.
I imagine him flying away as I contemplate
what it truly means to vanish.

As the rain becomes heavy, he becomes still.
Frozen in his gaze, flirting with my anticipated descriptions.
Oh, stoic prince, will you caw again?
Perhaps somewhere else,
where flowers do not need watering.

You soar now from the line,
like a wrestler leaping from the ropes,
leaving the taught cable in a wobble.
And then it stops, and you are gone
to shake your feathers over flowers
somewhere a little further down the road.

Sea Glass Dogs

And who do we blame for the pine trees
whose roots dangle over red cliffs,
pleading with the earth through countless storms
before collapsing into the dirt?

Certainly not our children, whose careful feet
explore hot sand and pointy rocks;
the children who search for sea glass,
leaving the little pieces to wither into nothing more
than scattered sparkles on sunny sand.

The high tide stones go unforaged,
though the beach's most beautiful pieces
lay beneath weathered sandstone and sun-dried shells.
Forgotten like old dogs at kennels,
their treasure is buried behind glass tears
that hide the eyes from the June sun…

I am awakened by the waves
and the sound of a fishing boat that
fades into the mainland mountains.
I wonder what more I must discover,
as I call to say I'll be late again for dinner.

Beetle on its Back

We have some design flaws, I think,
as a beetle falls on his back,
legs reaching t'ward heaven
for a helping hand.
I don't help right away.
I study his wasted movements
in hopes of learning something of us both.
Part of me hopes he can figure it out on his own.
He circles like a clock, ahead of schedule;
faulty mechanics, I think.
If only he could reach the edge of the table
I'm sure he could take flight.
How vulnerable to be belly up
in a world where so many are hungry.

3 AM

Have you ever woken up
in the middle of the night this way?
Splashed cold water on your face?
Stuck your head in the freezer?
Stood outside in your underwear
and gave into the moon?

If I could cry, there'd be a river,
but everything is frozen,
and it's too rough to skate.
So, I wait for the thaw,
in awe of the relief
that follows grief,
as cold water dribbles
from my smile.

This Beautiful Life

It really feels like a mountain
and I don't even know what's on top.
All I know is that there's a boot
that keeps kicking me down,
and I keep climbing.
Sometimes I fall lower
than I can ever remember being.
And I don't know if I climb
to reach the top, or because
I'm scared of what's at the bottom.

The force of the wind brings me to
the floor, and I wait for it to pass.
I've been in storms before.
They're more severe when you're on this path alone.
But you're never alone –

Falling rocks, dust in the eyes, painful releases –
I keep climbing.
I'm not alone here.
You've been kept awake by this,
brought to your knees by this,
lost your breath by this,
smiled through this,
cried through this,
stumbled through this,
soared through this –
gliding
in the stillness of colours,
and the softness of words.
Our sensitivities become
our greatest strengths.
This beautiful life.
This beautiful life.

Father's Wisdom

"Do as I say and not as I do."
I see now how unfair this command truly was.
For when I look back,
it's what you've done that I remember:

> The strength in your hug when the day was uncertain.

> The calm acceptance to make a change when a storm
> tried to pull you in.

> And the restraint found when anger reached a boil,
> to only hurt the man's shoe.

Grampy

What did my Grampy dream of when he was a boy?
I've only known him to wear button-down short sleeve shirts
that exposed a golden cross on a catcher's mound of chest hair.
I understand now the need for quick access to Jesus.

When I visited, I could always count on a full box of Lego
or being called by the names of my uncles and cousins
until Mary, knitting in her rocking chair, would say,
"Max. It's Max, Lorne."

The things that stick with me most,
are the smells found within our hugs –
spearmint gum, and Aqua Velva.
I never thought of what my father might have smelled
during the harder years.

Grampy quit drinking but he never stopped fighting the devil,
and by the time he laid down his gloves, I'd say they were even.
When that day came, I carried his casket,
with every tired muscle I could muster.

And just like that, the angels sang
for a man who loved with every piece of his heart
that he knew was there.

Victoria Park Sonnet

Rows of trees with bushy white blossoms
As though they were covered with snow
Line the path into the woods
That tells us where to go

Young men paint the city pool
Before the school year's through
A mother bends to teach her child
Just what her hands can do

A woman, nearly widowed
Sees the sky without a smile
And searches deep to find asleep
A tired little child

And with a yawn, she wakes again
With laughter in her eyes
To dry the tears from all the years
She's spent under the sky

When You Became a Tree

You took your lumps
through trembling breath
and rose again, a battered wonder.
Little did they know,
the tears would help grow
your union with the flowers.

The gophers nuzzled up against
your garden-rooted thighs.
Their tickled drunken stomachs
shined a light through darkened eyes.

Finches built a nest between
your ears with twigs they'd found;
a crown of stillness worn from bodies
rooted to the ground.

And when you were the oak
you never asked, "what can I give?"
Nor worried of what words to speak,
my love, you merely lived!

So, when I see those hammers
beating down in summer rain,
I'll send a poem into the home
where we will meet again.

Postcard House

There's a house being built on top of the hill.
Today I can see through the window;
the dining room, I presume.
Dreams become tangible
through orange-stained plywood.
I look through that window and see
the deepest greens and the brightest blues.
And the wooden border
captures the scene as a postcard.
I'll send it to you, and perhaps
one day we can live there;
myself, for the second time.

PEI

Where everyone is a meteorologist,
blinkers are optional,
potholes are deeper than Simmon's pool
and there's always something "going around."

Where a year without cruise ships,
and potatoes plagued with wart
can really turn the wheels of worry.
But a benefit for a friend in need
will bring out a love like no other.

Where the bridge toll rises with the sea level,
and they charge you to swim at the beach
unless you're "just going to Richard's"
(though the greatest treasures are found on hidden shores).

Where writers, painters, dancers, and musicians
peer beyond the fluttering maple leaves,
and fishermen sell their daily catch
from the backs of their trucks
in drug store parking lots.

Where ceilidhs and church picnics
bring out toe-tappers and toonie treasures
with lobster rolls and carnival ponies.
And we drink 'cause it's hot.
And we drink 'cause it's cold.

And whenever we leave,
we're proud to share tales
of a home that will always
have us back.

Early May Morning

when you can smell the sun
and the blue sky is a canvas
where jets paint white lines
for aerial highways
that dissolve into
Florida orange sunsets;
where forest green fills the empty stomach
of winter's melting hunger;
where jackhammers alter
the birdsong of paper starlings,
precisely cut to the shape of night,
when city cab drivers play online casinos
between the cracks of the steering wheel.

And you bask in your brilliance
and feign your foolishness
before awakening to vows of abstinence
that last nearly six hours, or until
you get a call from your best friend,
when you can go back to sleep
and share the dream all over again.

Dandelion

In my mind, I'm reading Leonard Cohen at the park.
Dandelions peak like the sun through fields of dead clouds.
A passage jumps off the page,
"You'd sing too, if you found yourself in a place like this."

Now sunlight dries a rainy day,
and morning dewdrops long to stay,
and yellow weeds turn into wine.
Fermented thoughts, they cross my mind.

And in the sun, my staggered song
will find the wish when days are long
to come back to this place we've known
and show it just how much we've grown.

Poverty by Choice?

I join the ranks of the unemployed
while new friends justify their poverty
as a deliberate choice;
as though it were something
nobody else could do.

Meanwhile, the real poor
hide their souls behind dirty cars
as capitalist hippies calculate
the ROI of their love
and mothers shriek
to see the cycle repeated.

An aimless saunter has its edge
and you will be burned
building a bridge
over a sea of fire.

Loyalty

The comfort of my loyalty
makes me want to challenge it.
In this generation, there is greater access
to deceit than rain.

We bring our lies into boxing rings
and beg for truth to be beaten out,
but more often than not,
we just hear the bell.

And our bruised lies swell
so we cover them up
with bandages and memories,
not letting the blood run
where it will.

Pride becomes the scars of
wounds we were afraid to let bleed,
cleaned quickly with yesterday's rain.

The Actor

You look at me
and I see the stillness
in your contemplation;
undressing the threat
of what I could be.
Your lingering gaze
awakens butterflies
from their bundled slumber
as orange wings flutter
down
and
down
again.
I watch them pull your costume away;
succumbing to your suspicion
at last.

For God

Blood drips from a jagged cut,
and gives me proof of your existence.
Please show me how to stay
within your arms
without coming so close
to death.

Twenty Years for Nothing

Timmies run before the funeral;
it's a wonder you even showed.

The Farmers

Heart in the fire, only getting stronger.
Days in the field, only getting longer.
We work, regardless of the harvest
or the yield of our field.

Ground will freeze and love can burn,
and lessons take some time to learn.
But you are a closing tulip,
and I am the evening sun;
not powerful enough to keep you in bloom
when the day's work is done.

Showcase

The delegates walk through tourist towns,
wined and dined by presidents that shuttle
their hangovers into breakfast buffets.
"Listen to this! Exquisite!" they say,
as a folk trio sings to cold scrambled eggs.

And mandolins trill in frozen lakes
as if baiting a hook to cast into the shadow of ice.
And emerging artists wait for an empty promise
of a mainland gig

sometime next year.

Memories of Wood

And I took Robert Frost's advice
as I walked through the woods,
but only until I reached the demolition site
where, just two summers before,
the men tore down the old nursing home.

And I thought of the song I wrote at the time;
you could call it a demo.

*"Brick by brick the building falls,
the same as it was made.
Blue sky wears a cloud of dust,
a particle parade."*

When I reached this memory
I turned around and moved
towards the ball diamonds
where fiddleheads played
to the crackle of a wooden bat.
Unlike that of a beachside bonfire
where once sounded the symphony
of bubbling springs
and nine o'clock crickets
with tiny rosined bows.

Birch, oak, and maple –
valiant soldiers standing guard
for the rising pollen
as though passing clouds
from a late August haiku.

It took me five years to realize
that I wasn't Charles Bukowski.
Some trees are dead
but remain standing
for some time.

The Sea Glass Collector

Sea foam teardrop;
inconsiderate smoothing
by great waves,
sandpaper beds
and stories imagined.

Ebbs and flows
on journeys home;
a sweet prize
for the candy
glass collector
and her
concealed
location.

Flecks of white
seaside impressions
carefully examined.
Stories of rum-runners,
dumpsites, and
other moonlight activities
yielding forbidden treasure.

Careful eyes to spot
a softened edge
where gentle thumbs
confirm the vision

only to be placed
in vases, unshattered
by an Eastern window.

The Sound to Soothe the Worried Mind

All this time I've yet to find
the sound to soothe the worried mind;
a ripple in a gentle wave,
something simple, something brave.
The clouds, they turn the water grey;
I'm grateful for them every day.
When skies turn blue, perhaps I'll find
the sound to soothe the worried mind.

Come to grips, it's just a script
that's written for the soul imprisoned.
Wisdom says I've broken free,
now all that's in the way is me.
Where rivers run and shadows hide,
where everything but love subsides,
when skies turn blue, perhaps I'll find
the sound to soothe the worried mind.

Psilocybin Sonnet

Primrose lilacs, summer dress
Interrupt my roving thoughts
Sunset orange, calm surrender
budding branches, worries lost

Hands extend like fire foam
watered when you need them most
Egyptian winds can topple tombs
belonging to the holy ghost

In so far the spirit finds me
speaking to a sacred cow
Dropping knowledge into pastures
Bastard be to pick them now

Brain confronts a frightful wish
as birds in paintings start to sing
Crying to a popcorn ceiling
Feeling tears only truth can bring

All along it was your nurturing soul
to which I would agree
To share a dance of love each day
with all that's left of me

Bonshaw Trail

Behold the behemoths
in Canadian forests
whose hollow temples
hold the woodpecker's secrets
while hummingbirds suck sugar
from budding bushes.

In this life you must be
as bold as a mosquito
and as timid as a deer.
Afterall, blood is blood,
and who am I to deny
someone's dinner?

The Hunted Crow

Timid black talons
on yellow Spring shingles.
Peeking over the gutter as
you contemplate a safer nesting
in a tree outside of range
from the neighbour's kids'
BB gun.

Beach Bonfire

Fire on a full moon, crackling twigs
Fiddlers call waves to the shore with their jigs
Love songs and stories passed 'round with the beer
Catching a glance and drawing her near.

Puffing cigars like harmonica tunes
Musical embers float over the dunes
The laughter is another wondrous sound
As marram grass sways and bends all around

We're nothing more than transferable dust!
Drunk and naked on the crust
Portable love in an overflowed cup
Dancing, sometimes throwing up

There's an unwritten beach and bonfire code:
No one gets too high, no one gets too low
No yearning for yesterday, no longing for tomorrow
And no woe can go uncured by the bottle

Musical River

Flowing through my day
like the waves at Peggy's Cove.
You used to say, "There's beauty in the ocean
even though it can drown a man."

Have you ever let the water get a word in?
It's the voice that often finds no ears.
But if one day you choose to listen,
it will share, with you, its song.

Every rushing wave, a melody.
Every salty drop, a lifetime.
Every glistening ripple,
a gentle reminder of your legs
wrapped around my waist
in this musical river.

Milton Acorn's Crows

I sit with the spawn
of Milton Acorn's crows
on a rotted tree stump
with wet April snow

I pack up a ball
bullseye on the oak
and listen to slush roads
and tires they soak

It's much too cold
for ants in my boots
or long conversations
and the thawing of roots

but this morning, Baba Ram Dass
put my mind at ease
This wisdom in laughter
I share with the trees

Bare as they wait
for the melting of snow
To turn into fountains
for the spawn of
Milton Acorn's crows

Cry Out for Love

Sadly, years will pass
with wealth amassed,
scores unsettled,
love unrealized,
and kindness jammed
into bottles of potential.
Anything to avoid
talking about personal pain.
The word "trauma" thrown around
like baseballs at batting practice.
Painted canvases of timid virtue
and lost minds.
Vines with poison flowers –
the most beautiful you've seen.
There are still some traps
in this world for the poets
and babies who cry out for love.

Whistling in a Battlefield

I can make a life out of melody and words;
you're telling me the birds do the same?
When a puddle becomes a bathtub
and signatures fade into wet ink,
your word becomes folklore for the children
of third generation corporate moguls.

How does the doctor feel
when he must be the subject of a prostate exam?
Timid?
Jealous?
Joyful?

So, we write out our fears
to gain courage over the wrecks
you never hear about on the news;
the internal wars never televised;
the aching revolutions we carry
into coffee shop counters
where armour is donned until dusk –
where tears will rust
the so-called silver of the day.

Admiring You

You sit at the kitchen table almost every night
after working with the children all day.
Your failed year of sobriety
pours into our only wine glass
which is also our only beer glass,
but you've never been one
to judge the shape of another;
only that of yourself.

Your mind hasn't caught up to your bladder
as you rock back and forth on the chair.
It begins as a suggestion,
then becomes an emergency.
And my eyes give away my thoughts
'cause you say, "What's so funny?"
as you leap towards the bathroom.
And I can't narrow it down to just one thing;
it's some combination of your urgent dancing
with a timely reminder of Newton's Third Law.

And I admire your capacity for work
but I admire your tears more
as you wash them away in the bathtub.
My own tears falling backwards
down my throat.

Silly of them, really.
For I know the air is kind
and so are you.

Poetry is

the look you give me
when we're sitting on the couch
and you're ready for me
to leave your imagination.

An Old Friend

I walk by that bus on half-moon nights,
and think of the music we're not playing.
And the song doesn't come on,
but I recall the melody
like an old friend
who's left town
but not my heart.

Of all the wasted years,
those were my favourite.

Blockage

Love is the laxative
for a constipated heart.

Leaving the Band

I grew weary of red wine and Ritalin chalices
during ring ceremonies when I fell back into
traditional versions of monogamy.
The wasted awe during cannonball sunsets
became enough to ring the doorbell to the little boy
living in a forgotten world of unhealed memories.

My convictions were swayed by
my own perception of the missing piece
to my unconditional love.
All the mushrooms and songs
became painful reminders
of a better life left behind.

What do we do with these beasts
that never cease to offer the open plains?
When do we ride those horses again?
But again, none of these questions matter
when you trade in a forest fire for a birthday candle.

Evening cigar

burning like a small midnight volcano after the poetry reading.
Like the cigar, I feel accomplished and empty
as I look at the tombstones that no longer remind me of mortality.
Let your soul, lost as it may be, find its vibration.
Ride it like the cocaine sweat
that falls from the brow of James Brown.
When he says "I feel good!" you believe it.
Let them call you crazy so long as they believe you.
I wish that flame still burned inside of me instead of
the smoke from old dreams that never caught fire.
Four, five, six stars arrive in the sky, all at once,
and I remember again not who I am, but where.
And for tonight, that's enough.

Island Summer

Oh, Island summer
and your promise of adventure.
Tempting us to break our vows
of not working too many hours.
Tickling our overloaded senses
and granting a worry too soon
of what will fill the
Christmas stockings.

Let your rolling waves
rock us into submission
as singing sands
echo a purgatory tune
for ocean and dune.

Take our picture
as we give our bodies
to the summer music,
where pink shoulders
are only revealed after sunset,
for it's hard to see the damage
while it's being done.

Whisper our names
as we bathe in your stillness,
letting go of decorative bowls
filled with the severed heads
of provincial cowards.

Oh, Island summer,
the daylight and you,
now sinking beyond
each other's horizon
as moonlight guides
a storm somewhere else.

Ego Death

Cold winds blow my ego into
classrooms that have no walls,
parting ways with tradition,
set free from superstition.

Music is the sound of laughter
on a construction site, and
it's the shiver of October
on an apartment balcony.

Sing from the richness of your soul's fountain
where the heart and mind are free to splash and swim
and duck underwater for refreshing silence
whenever they wish.

Let the ego bow, as if to exit the stage
on which it has been performing;
as if to leave the theatre
to which it's been clinging.

How dare I say the book is finished
without a season like this?

The Dunes

Manicured plots
beyond pretension;
a careful peace,
a considerate joy.

All of the beautiful people
with knowing smiles
gather beside evening windows
to watch bloodsuckers near
the nectared centers
of yellow donuts.

The wood carvings wear
their weathered strength,
tested by winter winds
where water trickles from
the mouths of
Hindu goddesses.

When we walk beside the peonies
and drink the ginger soup,
we are home.

When we envision the paintings
in corridors untravelled
and laugh at Polaroids unshaken,
we are home.

When we find a friendly acquaintance,
who will never be more than such,
though in their eyes we see the shared world,
indeed, we are home.

And so, we take our bottled sunshine
with a single strike of lightning
and let it out slowly
to daring hares who dash
across National Park highways.

We sprinkle summer emeralds
through coastal forest paths,
where mosquitos know better
than to buzz beside our necks.

And as the sun sets, we fill our bottle
with its remaining magic
as warm sea water sloshes
around the walls of glass houses.

We wait until the osprey catches his fish
before returning, sandy-legged,
to a car that will hold onto the day
that we must now let drift away.

The Bird

Maybe today just isn't your day,
like a bird standing out in the drizzling rain.
But perhaps, in fact, the bird just laughs,
where you see despair, she sees a bath.

Falling Music

The snowflakes are falling
like soft piano;
each fresh layer of powder
is a song.
Ivory-tickled icing sugar
in C major,
with the occasional shadow,
sharp as the beak of a bluejay,
striking the chords of darkness.
Cold, abysmal winter
with wooden trunks
of possibility.
And though his body
no longer needs the nourishment,
we set his place at the table
as the music falls,
soft as snowflakes.

Winter Closure

And so, should this be my final account
of all things beautiful,
roll me in the first powdered snow
like a jelly donut.
Fasten me safely in a Christmas light.
Save me the space between the branches
where I can join the wind in its Northern song.
Look to the grey sky as though it is but one cloud
that calls our eyes forward to look
at the angels who now walk beside us.

ABOUT THE AUTHOR

Lawrence Maxwell is a Prince Edward Island writer. His joy for writing began in elementary school, penning a series of short stories surrounding a central character, "Oddey the Mouse." In early adulthood, he began to focus on music, winning the 2019 Music PEI Country Album of the Year for his debut album Not Your Outlaw. His sophomore album, Almost Natural was also a Music PEI award winner and was nominated for an ECMA in 2021. Poetry has always gone hand in hand with Lawrence's music. His debut poetry collection, Morning Spoon, was shortlisted for the 2022 PEI Island Literary Awards, and his recent poem, "Poppy's Handshake" was the winner of the Off Topic poetry contest for May 2022. His most recent published works include two poems selected for the Canadian League of Poets "Poetry Pause" edition.

4 † $

Made in the USA
Columbia, SC
06 August 2023